Psychological Terrorism!

Discrimination,

Harassment,

Retaliation in the Workplace!

Michael P. Brown

Copyright © 2015 by Michael P. Brown.

All rights reserved.

No part of this publication may be reproduced, stored in a retrieval system, or transmitted in any form or by any means—electronic, mechanical, photocopy, recording, or any other—without the prior permission of the author, except as provided by USA copyright law.

Contents

Preface 4

Laws and Legalities 23

Chapter 1: Segregation 27

Chapter 2: Favoritism 32

Chapter 3: Stereotyping 35

Chapter 4: Harrasment 37

Chapter 5: Attempted Murder with Depraved Indifference 43

Chapter 6: Sexual Harassment 45

Chapter 7: Slave Labor/Wage and Hour Violations .. 47

Chapter 8: Extortion Conspiracy 49

Chapter 9: Psychological Terrorism and Torture 51

Chapter 10: Organized Real Estate Crimes 53

Glossary 74

Preface

DFEH Case #238332-101141-R

I, Michael Brown, hereby charge Chevron Corporation, its personnel, Staffmark Group, LLC, United Steel Workers Local 5, and the Red Wing Brands of America, INC, with a series of civil, constitutional, and international offenses. These alleged crimes were committed against me during my tenure as an employee of the Staffmark agency while assigned to contractor duties at the Chevron Oil Refinery in Richmond, California.

From May 2011 to January 2014, I was subjected to:

- Two years and six months of segregation
- Favoritism
- Profiling
- Stereotyping
- Harassment
- Depraved indifference
- Attempted murder

- Sexual harassment

- Slave labor

- Wage and hour violations

- Extortion

- Conspiracy

- Terrorism

- Psychological terrorism/torture

- Slavery

- Kickbacks

- Violations of the RICO Act (racketeering)

- Discrimination

These offenses resemble the Jim Crow Laws, which were in effect from 1876 to 1965 and were deemed unconstitutional, yet seemed to persist in 2014 at the Chevron Oil Refinery. Such tactics are also reminiscent of the Willie Lynch letter on the creation of a slave. Today, these methods have evolved into what is termed psychological terrorism, torture, and warfare—insidious means of breaking a person's spirit.

For further information on the Willie Lynch letter, one might refer to the "willie lynch final call" on Google. The Geneva/UN Conventions strictly prohibit torture, coercion, and abuse. Article 3 of the Geneva Conventions specifically bans acts of "violence to life and person," including murder, mutilation, cruel treatment, torture, and acts that are degrading or violate personal dignity. Meanwhile, Article 4 of the European Convention on Human Rights forbids slavery, servitude, and forced labor. Article 10 mandates that all individuals deprived of their freedom must be treated with humanity and respect for their inherent dignity. War crime tribunals hold the accused accountable without offering an opportunity for forgiveness.

Dated: June 25, 2014

Psychological Terrorism: Discrimination, Harassment, and Retaliation in the Workplace

April 4, 2014

The Pervasive Subculture of Abuse, Harassment, Discrimination, and Wrongful Termination in the Workplace:

I have recently provided you with all the pertinent documents highlighting the abuse, harassment, and discrimination I endured at the Chevron establishment. My wrongful termination was a direct result of standing up for myself. Whenever a transgression was made against me, I consistently addressed the issue during our breaks and lunchtime in the break room. I even escalated my concerns to our supervisor, Stan Deloran, who unfortunately turned a deaf ear to my pleas. Stan repeatedly told me, "The union worker is your boss, and you must comply with his directives." I had to assert multiple times that Staff Mark, the agency that placed me at Chevron's oil refinery, was my actual employer. If there were any grievances, they should be directed at Staff Mark.

I also experienced various forms of harassment and discrimination for not conforming to what Stan Deloran described as the union and Chevron's traditions. On one occasion, when I didn't immediately respond to a filler named Kazi, he claimed that Stan wanted to see me. In my discussion with Stan, I tried to clarify my role. I posited that I was there to aid the drum production line, suggesting that perhaps I was the filler's helper. When Stan negated this, I suggested I might be his assistant, but this too was denied. I then offered that I might be a contractor supporting the filler in production, but Stan rejected this as well. It left me questioning my exact position. Moreover, he made an absurd claim, stating that if I needed to use the restroom, I could only do so after completing the orders or upon obtaining the filler's permission.

Every injustice I suffered is meticulously documented in the papers I've shared with you. Since my unjust dismissal on January 31, 2014, I've been unemployed. I appreciate your attention to this matter. Thank you.

Dated: August 31, 2014

DFEH Case #238332-113927

Violation of Human Rights and Contraventions of Civil/International Law

This pertains to the violation of the prohibition against torture and other cruel, inhuman, or degrading treatment, as articulated in Article 1 of the UN Convention against Torture. The subsequent transgressions were executed against me by Cynthia Mata and Gerry Reyes, both representatives of the Department of Fair Employment and Housing (DFEH): conspiracy, accessory after the fact, obstruction of justice, tampering with public records, and violation of the Department of Fair Employment Housing Act. Notably, *Article 14 of this act includes a prohibition against discrimination.

It's essential to clarify that there exist myriad forms of discrimination and harassment, many of which have remained uncommunicated to you. These issues extend far beyond conventional understandings. For instance, discrimination or harassment may arise because of a lively and fun-loving personality that isn't shared by peers, or perhaps due to one's carefree lifestyle. Indeed, any trace of negativity can be grounds for discrimination, particularly in professional settings.

Given our membership in the United Nations, we must recognize that any form of discrimination is unequivocally impermissible. The United Nations has a set constitution that all members must adhere to. Also implicated in this scenario are the European Court of Human Rights, War Crimes Tribunal, and the Geneva Conventions. These entities collectively decree that if justice remains elusive within your home country, recourse to international courts is an available and valid pathway.

To my dismay, I unearthed the disturbing fact that instead of assisting me in my quest for justice, there seemed to be a conspiracy against me, aiming to deny me my basic human rights in this modern age.

To contextualize, on April 3, 2014, I lodged a complaint with the DFEH, flagging the infringement of my human and constitutional rights by four corporations and their staff. Accompanying this was a comprehensive fifty-one-page document delineating the discrimination, harassment, and retaliation I endured. The lead investigator assigned to this case was Cynthia Mata. Following the submission of my complaint, I was given the assurance of being contacted within ten days for an interview. However, as April 13 rolled around, no call materialized.

Opting to be patient, considering the volume of

my submission, I waited until April 24, 2014, before reaching out to DFEH. During this interaction, a representative named Krista relayed that my complaint had been erroneously filed as 'inactive' and, as a result, remained unreviewed. I was then promised a correction and a subsequent interview with Cynthia Mata within ten days. Yet again, this deadline lapsed with no communication.

It wasn't until June 3, 2014, that Cynthia contacted me, initiating the long-awaited interview. Shockingly, she confessed to not having reviewed my complaint or the accompanying document, citing its loss. Furthermore, she confirmed that no investigative actions had been undertaken, and no documents had been exchanged with any parties implicated in the complaint.

"I pointed out, "It's inconceivable because I already received an email from you dated April 14, 2014. This email contained the original complaint form I submitted on April 3, 2014. Not only did you commence and conclude the investigation, but you also verified the instances of discrimination, harassment, and retaliation with my witness, Terrence Thomas, on April 14, 2014, at the Chevron Oil Refinery in Richmond, California. I received this verification the very same day. However, when I reviewed the DFEH complaint form with its verification, I noticed some details were deliberately omitted from the 'statement of facts' section. Furthermore, during the filing process, there was a provision to send personal notes exclusively for the case investigator's eyes. This was also absent from the 'statement of facts' section."

The undeniable truth is that they had received my fifty-one-page document, holding onto it from April 3, 2014, to June 3, 2014. This amounts to sixty days in their possession. Both Krista and Cynthia Mata, along with the DFEH, have seemingly tried to obstruct my path to justice, making them, and by extension the Department of Fair Employment and Housing, complicit in this conspiracy against my human rights.

Krista did mention that my complaint was relegated to an inactive file. However, this implies someone had to have seen it because one would need to view the data on their computer monitor to process or alter it. When Cynthia Mata contacted me on June 3, 2014, and I inquired if she had perused my complaint and accompanying documents, she claimed my file had been lost. But how is that plausible? Especially since I had conversed with Krista on April 24, 2014, and she confirmed the necessary corrections were made. Moreover, I received the original complaint form via email on April 14, 2014, which clearly stated that Terrence Thomas, a supervisor at Chevron Oil Refinery in Richmond, California, had verified my allegations of discrimination, harassment, and retaliation as true.

Thus, Cynthia Mata, on behalf of the Department of Employment and Housing, stands accused of conspiracy, accessory after the fact, obstruction of justice, and tampering with public records (specifically, the creation, presentation, or filing of a false document as per N.J.S.A.2C:28-7a (2)). Notably, *Article 14 stresses the prohibition against discrimination, while *Article 75 strictly forbids acts such as murder and all forms of torture, be they physical or mental.

DFEH Case #238332-101141-R

The reason Cynthia Mata could conduct, complete, and receive verification from my witness all on 4/14/2014 was because, two months before I lodged my complaint, I had provided copies of my documents to Staffmark, Chevron, the Union, and Red Wing. Given the gravity of the situation, they were presumably instructed to be truthful. It was at this juncture that a conspiracy against me seems to have been hatched. Please note: this is merely a summary.

I have over sixty pages and possess the necessary documents to substantiate my claims. Justice was denied to me by Cynthia Mata and Gerry Reyes of the California Civil Rights Department, formerly known as the Department of Fair Employment and Housing. Additionally, Chris Green from the EEOC declined to provide me the federal right-to-sue forms. Despite having effectively secured my case, individuals like Chris Green, Mary Bonilla, and Deborah Randa from the EEOC withheld the requisite forms from me. I attempted to reach a settlement, but later uncovered a conspiracy aimed at infringing upon my human rights. I can furnish all the documents you might need to understand this better. Moreover, I was wrongfully dismissed on 1/31/2014.

Discussing the pervasive subculture of harassment, discrimination, and wrongful termination in workplaces: Hello, how are you? Since my termination on January 31, 2014, I haven't been employed. Unexpectedly one evening, I received a call from Laura Trevino, a representative from Staffmark. She conveyed that the vice president of Chevron was displeased with my comments, even though I was merely defending myself against repeated injustices. Her directive was for me to remain at home until things were sorted out. Naturally, I raised a concern: without work, how was

I expected to sustain myself? Staffmark, as a form of compensation, continued to pay me, given that I was still technically under contract to work for Chevron.

There was no legitimate reason barring me from my job — I hadn't been suspended, laid off, or terminated for any transparent cause. By keeping me away from work without a clear reason, Staffmark essentially committed an infringement. It's perplexing: how could they compensate me for work when I wasn't even performing my duties? Since that episode, neither Staffmark nor Chevron have reintegrated me, leaving me without a consistent income source. As bills accumulate, I refuse to be deprived of basic sustenance due to their apparent guilt or discomfort in facing me.

Staffmark already possesses a copy of the documents I plan to share with you. In forthcoming emails, I'll elucidate the maltreatments I've endured. Originally, Staffmark seemed amenable to assisting me against the other parties. However, as time progressed, I discerned a reluctance on their part — potentially an attempt to protect their interests given their possible involvement. There's a likelihood Staffmark communicated with the other entities and disseminated my documents, though I can't confirm this.

I thought it might be pertinent to inform you that the documents might have been shared with others, though I cannot say this with certainty.

For further details, you can contact the following:

- Staffmark onsite: (510) 242-1821. Please reach out to Laura Trevino.

- Staffmark Corporation: (614) 475-2250, Human Resources Department.

- Chevron Refinery onsite: (510) 242-3493 / (510) 242-3324. You can contact either Stan Deloran or Terrance Thomas.

- Chevron Oil Corporation: 1.888.825.5247, Human Resources Department.

Please note the multiple DFEH case numbers:

- #238322101141-R: Michael Brown vs. Laura Trevino of Staffmark.

- #238332-115622: Michael Brown vs. Cynthia Mata of the Department of Fair Employment and Housing concerning violations of the Fair Housing Act.

- EEOC charge number: 37A-2014-00743C

- FEPA charge number: 238332-113927.

Psychological Context: I aim to draw parallels between the psychological techniques used for oppression and torture by Willie Lynch and the psychological trauma I endured at the Chevron Oil Refinery over a span of two years and six months. While my experiences did not involve physical torture instruments like whips, chains, or branding irons, there were two distinct instances where I believe there was an attempt on my life by contaminating coffee in the packaging break room upstairs.

Reference to International Law: Geneva Conventions' Article 3 explicitly condemns "violence to life and person."

Historical Context: Willie Lynch, a slave master from the 1700s, devised a calculated psychological method to subdue the spirit of enslaved individuals, subsequently giving rise to the term 'Negro'. In today's vernacular, these tactics are recognized as forms of psychological terrorism, torture, and warfare. For a deeper understanding, you can search for the "Willie Lynch letter" online.

Sociological Insight: In the modern workplace, notably at the Chevron Oil Plantation, there persists a subculture of abuse, harassment, and discrimination. Since the advent of employment structures, where one individual works for another, there has unfortunately been an unwritten expectation by some. These individuals believe that merely performing well, adhering to safety protocols, and maintaining harmonious relations with colleagues isn't sufficient. They impose an additional, unofficial demand: the expectation for employees to tolerate their harassment and abuse, essentially reducing them to subservient roles or, metaphorically, to slaves.

African people were brought to America in the 1500s, shackled in chains. Now, in the twenty-first century, certain elements of that dark past seem to be re-emerging, as I've personally experienced. It is evident that employees at the Chevron Oil Refinery exhibit psychopathic behavior—a personality type characterized by antisocial and often criminal actions, devoid of moral responsibility or social conscience. Such behavior equates to war crimes.

DFEH Case #238332-101141-R

Torture, as defined by Article 1 of the UN Convention Against Torture, constitutes crimes against humanity. The following lists the war crimes allegedly committed by Chevron Oil, Staffmark, the

Union, and the Red Wing Shoes Corporation in violation of both US and International laws:

International Courts, Conventions, Covenants, and Articles that Chevron, Staffmark, the Union, and Red Wing Shoes are accused of violating:

1. The Human Rights Council

2. International Bill of Human Rights

3. Geneva Conventions

4. Convention for the Protection of Human Rights and Fundamental Freedoms, amended by Protocol No. 11, including Protocol Nos. 1, 4, 6, 7, 12, and 13

5. Convention Against Torture and Other Cruel, Inhuman, or Degrading Treatment or Punishment (CAT)

6. American Convention on Human Rights O.A.S. Treaty Series No. 36, 1144 U.N.T.S. 123

7. The International Criminal Court (I.C.C.)

8. International Covenant on Civil and Political Rights (ICCPR)

9. International Covenant on Economic, Social,

and Cultural Rights

10. International Covenant on Civil and Political Rights (articles 7 & 10)

11. United Nations Convention Against Torture

12. European Convention on Human Rights

13. The Universal Declaration of Human Rights, specifically:

- Article 17

- Article 27

14. Color of Law Act. 18 U.S.C. section 242

15. 18 U.S.C. section 245 and 42 U.S.C. section 1983

16. European Convention on Human Rights

Any individual convicted under these acts can face imprisonment for up to twenty years per court conviction, or even the death penalty, as stipulated by the United Nations Convention Against Torture.

DFEH Case #238332-101141-R

I am formally stating my intention to seek a settlement. Should there be a lack of cooperation, I am prepared to turn to CNN, Court TV, YouTube, and any other available platforms with a wide reach. Could you ensure that Chevron, the Union, and Red Wing receive a copy of this document?

Psychological Note: If this case goes to trial centered on allegations of abuse, harassment, and discrimination, it would allow me to introduce evidence related to these issues. Their attempts to reduce my status resemble dehumanizing practices from historical eras, akin to forcing someone into servitude. I would then be able to present the court with various video clips demonstrating abuse, harassment, and discrimination to depict what certain Chevron employees tried to impose on me.

Regarding jury selection, it's virtually impossible to assemble a group of twelve jurors without at least one who can empathize with my experience. A single dissenting juror can have a significant impact. Moreover, the longer the case remains in the media spotlight, the more public opinion may shift, especially once the media delves deep into the matter. Exposure of such behavior on a global platform would resonate with many who have undergone similar experiences. This creates a platform—a forum—for those who've been abused, harassed, or discriminated against to share and express their feelings. All this turmoil could have been circumvented if individuals did not operate under the illusion that their job position or any other factor gives them the right to mistreat another human being.

Laws and Legalities

1. Title VII of the Civil Rights Act, as amended, protects employees and job applicants from employment discrimination based on race, color, religion, sex and national origin.

2. The Civil Rights Act of 1991.

3. 2403 Hobbs Act Extortion by Force Violence or fear

4. Extortion in California is a crime described in Section 518 of the California Penal Code.

5. Wage Theft Protection Act

6. California code Section 487m - Wage theft; grand theft

7. California Labor Code section 201,

8. Title VII of the Civil Rights Act of 1964

9. 42 U.S. Code § 2000e–2 - Unlawful employment practices

10. Profiling

11. ARTICLE 1. Unlawful Practices, Generally California Government Code Section 12950

12. (Depraved Indifference) Penal Law § 120.25

13. CM-618 Segregating, Limiting, and Classifying Employees

14. Nepotism, Cronyism, & Favoritism:

15. 18 USC § 1514(d)(1) Harassment

16. California Fair Employment and Housing Act or FEHA) Discrimination Harassment, Retaliation

17. Government Code §12940(k) Discrimination/Harassment

18. 29 CFR § 1604.11 - Sexual harassment

19. 29 CFR § 1606.8 - Harassment.

20. California Fair Employment Practices Act

21. California Government Code Sec. 12950.1

Abusive Conduct

22. Public Entity Liability California Government Code Sections 815-818.9 Article 2.

23. 18 United States Code Section 241 Conspiracy

24. 18 United States Code Section 242 Deprivation of Rights

25. 18 United States Code Section 245 Federally Protected Activities

26. 42 United States Code Section 1983 Right to Sue

27. 42 United States Code Section 1985 Conspiracy to Interfere with Civil Rights

28. 42 United States Code Section 1986 Action for Neglect to Prevent

29. 38 Code of Federal Regulations Section 3.103 Procedural Due Process

30. Substantive Due Process/7th and 14th Amendments

Chapter 1: Segregation

DFEH Case #238332-101141-R

Upon starting my job, I was initially stationed at the jug-filling unit. There, a contractor named Ryan instructed me on overseeing the four machines. While our guidelines as contractors explicitly stated that we shouldn't press buttons, open machine cabinets, or place our hands inside since we weren't union machine operators, these very tasks were assigned to us.

Following my training with Ryan, the routine was straightforward: the person who completed their training would move to another station, allowing the newly trained individual to become the trainer. Thus, after absorbing what Ryan taught, I trained another contractor, affectionately termed "Little Doug." Ideally, I would have then moved to a different workstation, letting Doug assume the role of a trainer. However, instead of following this pattern, Doug was reassigned to the blending department shortly after Darby's departure. It was disheartening to witness Darby being mistreated, often becoming the butt of many jokes. People around were well aware of my stance against such behavior.

Despite my seniority among contractors, my role seemed stagnant. During this period, I undertook the responsibility of cleaning the entire packaging warehouse floor. It was around this time the refinery gained recognition as the top oil refinery in Richmond, California. This acclaim, however, led to my feeling of isolation from the main group.

During my tenure, I was involved in training several individuals, including Carlos and Rafael Rios Jr. — the latter being the son of a union worker who sexually harrassed me. I also trained Carlos's cousin, Christen. This brought the tally to four individuals I'd trained, yet my position remained unchanged. To add insult to injury, Christen was later promoted to the drum warehouse as a forklift operator — the exact role I was initially hired for. It became evident that while numerous contractors were being inducted into the drum warehouse, my transfer was consistently overlooked.

Occasionally, Felix Hernandez, the supervisor overseeing the drum warehouse forklift operators, would casually ask when I'd be joining his team. My standard response was that the decision was up to Stan Deloran. Each query to Stan resulted in vague replies, hinting at potential openings or the need for a Chevron-specific forklift test. Whenever the latter was mentioned, I would always reaffirm my readiness, citing my existing forklift certification- a prerequisite set by Staffmark. Surprisingly, despite Staffmark's longstanding association with the refinery, they failed to mention the necessity for an additional test.

Reflecting on my journey, it's deeply troubling to acknowledge the psychological trauma I endured. The harrowing experience of being treated less than human was both shocking and eye-opening, especially recognizing that such oppressive behavior has been rampant in workplaces for decades.

It's crucial for everyone to know the truth so that diligent, hardworking individuals understand their rights extend beyond common knowledge. In America, you possess constitutional rights, and internationally, you have protections under the United Nations and the European Court of Human Rights. If you believe your country's justice system has let you down, the law allows you to seek a hearing with the European Court of Human Rights.

After a lengthy nine months on the jug line, they promoted me to the drum line. However, I was still in packaging and the sole black man responsible for cleaning the floor. Roughly a year later, I was finally transferred to the drum warehouse, where I began additional forklift training. At last, I was executing the responsibilities I was initially hired for. However, around six weeks into this role, Stan Deloran informed me that the drum warehouse supervisor wished to speak with me. I learned there was an issue on the drum line that halted production. Even though I was a non-union contractor, I was puzzled about the sudden inefficiency of the union workers. It emerged that a union worker named Kazi felt overwhelmed by his workload. Furthermore, the contractor paired with Kazi, Jeremy, was unfamiliar with the drum conveyor machine's operation- a machine I had mastered over two years as a non-union contractor. Stan assured me this disruption was merely temporary and that I'd soon return to the drum warehouse. Once I rectified the drum line issue, I was recognized with an award for my exemplary service. However, contrary to Stan Deloran's assurances, I never returned to the drum warehouse. During my brief reassignment to packaging, they hired someone else for my initial position. Now, I find myself back in packaging, once again cleaning floors. To them, I felt reduced to just a "slave"- a black man devoid of basic human rights. This treatment exemplifies harassment and discrimination based on race.

Chapter 2: Favoritism

I regularly found myself training numerous new employees of the company, only for them to be transferred to the positions that I had worked hard for- hard enough that I could confidently say that I deserved to hold them. It was sickening. I would often witness them huddled in the corners of the warehouse, whispering amongst themselves. They attempted to treat the contractors like slaves. We were assigned to work alongside the union workers, but every time they had a project that involved very little work, they would end up replacing the contractor with one of their union buddies. Similarly, in instances where they had projects involving high levels of physical labor, they would have them be assigned to a contractor. This was unnerving to me, and I should know because I was the only contractor with the courage to stand up and fight for my rights as a human as well as an employee of the company.

Time after time, I observed them displaying clear favoritism toward their union friends, and even towards certain contractors who had proven themselves worthy of being included in their game. Some contractors would be allowed to engage in things that no one else was allowed to engage in, and even go into certain areas that were prohibited for everyone else. What added insult to injury, was that reporting these behaviors would change nothing. One would simply be ignored or given a project that no union worker wanted to do. I was the only one sweeping and mopping the warehouse floors for the duration of my time at Chevron Refinery in Richmond, California. No one was ever appointed or even asked to do it, except for me.

I remember one day at the plant—the workers were having a promotion party. There were about fifty people attending the function; and of course, we had the task of setting up tables and chairs. The odd thing, however, was that none of the union workers would even so much as lend a helping hand. Moreover, when it came to preparing the meal, no one was interested in cleaning the meat. Out of the goodness of my heart, I took up the gruelling task of cleaning over fifty pieces of meat, so that all the guests would enjoy a good lunch. Of course, when it was time to eat, everyone enthusiastically joined in to help. The real tragedy that had an impact on me, was that no one directed a word of appreciation my way, but they all thanked the people who set the lunch up.

Chapter 3: Stereotyping

They never created any rules relating to cleaning up after themselves. Instead, they plainly stated that it was a job for contractors to do. That indifference resulted in me cleaning the whole packaging warehouse floor for over two years! They made me the designated industrial custodian, so that every time something needed cleaning, I would be called.

They acted as though a black man was the only one who can clean a floor. In retrospect, I think they really believed this in their heart of hearts; because otherwise, why would Chevron allow this type of stereotyping to persist? I am fully aware that this shameful behavior did not start with me. For years, they have benefited from the profiling and stereotyping of black men, almost as if it was a basic policy at Chevron refineries. All of us have probably experienced being stereotyped and profiled on the job or know someone who has. An example of this can be when one is repeatedly told that they do a particular job so much better than the others, and no one can do it as well as them.

This, naturally, makes them feel great about themselves, which is completely normal. But with time they may come to realize that the unending praise for their good work may just be a trick to keep them doing that job, making sure they are deceived into never speaking up or stepping out of line. Ultimately, it becomes clear that the belief these supervisors hold, is that the job, as well as the person, are both beneath them.

It should be noted that psychological warfare is a scientifically studied process to manipulate and exploit someone using their good will or positive emotions against them, even going as far as making them believe that their own five senses are lying to them.

Chapter 4: Harrasment

One day, we received an order on the drum filling station, to fill over three hundred drums of oil at four hundred pounds per drum. I was given the job to process and prepare the drums for filling. The refinery is so large that we had to wear communication devices to maintain contact with each other. As I was unloading the drums onto the conveyer machine, I began receiving constant calls; but every time I would answer, it would either be silence on the other end or I would hear laughing in the background. On top of that was the fact that all communications in the refinery are monitored by the management, so they knew full well what was going on and failed to take any action against it.

Another day, I was mopping the warehouse floor, and some of the union workers were driving motorized vehicles. They wanted to drive over the wet floor, and I asked them to go another way. There were multiple dry areas for them to easily get to their destination, but they drove across the wet floor in spite of my concerns. When

I reported the incident, no one lifted a finger to help. The more I stood up for myself as a human being, the more unconstitutional crimes (Jim Crow Laws) and psychological terrorism they committed against me.

I have recently received another call from Cynthia Mata representing the Department of Fair Employment and Housing. She is the case manager assigned to investigate my complaint DEFH Case #238332-101141-R of discrimination, harassment, and retaliation. She is, once again, claiming that this is only the start of the interview process. Why is she subjecting me to this psychological torture? I reiterated to her that not only have I received prior verification from her, but also my complaint and the allegations of discrimination, harassment, and retaliation are true- and have been confirmed by the signature of the supervisor Terrence Thomas, on April 14, 2014, at Chevron Oil Refinery in Richmond, California. It seems to me that Cynthia Mata had been trying to sabotage my case from the start!

At this point, I, Michael Brown, had been the only man sweeping and mopping the entire packaging warehouse floor for the two years and six months of my tenure. Ou work crew in packaging consists of a mixture of different ethnic groups. Carlos and Mauricio are cousins, and Mexican. Jeremy is white, Alex is Asian, and Rafael Rios Jr., Christen, and George are Mexican; along with Carlos and Mauricio, who also happen to be cousins. The work crews are made up of nonunion contractors and the union workers who were assigned to aid in production. There is a particular union worker, by the name of Doug- or as we call him- big Doug. He's been a Chevron employee for over forty years. He used to give me standing ovations for how well I cleaned the floor, especially when the executives came to visit. Once I started cleaning, the company started receiving awards for being the number 1 refinery in North America, despite being regularly filthy at the time of my arrival. That seems to be one of the reasons why they singled me out to keep me doing that job. This is also why I was denied a good faith interactive process and the chance to advance in my career like my peers.

Whenever I asked Stan Deloran why I was the

only one cleaning; he said, "It is a tradition at Chevron and the union that the contractor must do what the union worker tells you no matter what, because we are your bosses. Chevron has polices in place to keep your area clean. That means everyone must clean." One time, he gave me an example, and the union worker Kazi, as previously mentioned, heard him. He said to me, "If you have to go to the bathroom but you still have orders to fill, you must wait until you finish the work or get permission from your union worker." That's harassment. And out of all the mixed ethnic groups, I was the only black man that Stan was always asking to clean. That's discrimination based on race. It is stereotyping, profiling, and favoritism.

I was hired before Carlos, Jeremy and the others but they got promoted to different jobs while I was still cleaning the floors in packaging warehouse. As a matter of fact, on many occasions I would be working in production, and Stan would pull me off of my assigned job to clean the floors- replacing me with a union worker. The whole packaging plant can verify that I was the only one cleaning the entire warehouse floor for the duration of two years and six months. When the plant received awards for cleaning, the whole plant knew that I was the only man to be credited for a job well done. It did not matter where I was assigned in packaging- whenever Stan Deloran wanted something cleaned, he only ever came to me.

There were several occasions when Stan would ask Terrence Thomas to bring me away from my assigned job, and make me clean something up for him. Whatever task I was working on, would of course be transferred to a union worker.

One particular day comes to mind- before my wrongful termination- when I was assigned to work with a union worker named Alex. I was monitoring the production machinery and lines when they started to back up. I figured out the problem and attempted to rectify the situation, but before I knew it, he began directing profanities at me; provoking me to ask him to watch his mouth. Alex then proceeded to run to Stan Deloran, declaring that I was not doing my job. I did attempt to explain to Stan that Alex was lying and my version of the events can be corroborated by checking the security camera footage. I elucidated that the recently installed cameras would clearly display that Alex was not telling the truth. However, instead of checking the security tapes, Stan took me off my assigned duties yet again, and put union worker George in my place- asking me to go back to cleaning. During this incident, Terrance Thomas was, once again, a witness, being present when I presented my case to Stan about Alex lying. What upsetted me even more was that Alex was well-aware of the presence of cameras recording us- he was just not fazed by it, knowing that he would get off the hook by creating a falsified sequence of events.

If that is not harassment and discrimination based on color, then I don't know what is. An investigation was conducted, which proved that I was indeed telling the truth. However, they conspired to deprive me of my human right for justice, rather than mend the situation.

Chapter 5: Attempted Murder with Depraved Indifference

One morning before work, I made some coffee, as was a daily habit of mine. During break, I went into the packaging break room. I poured out some coffee into my cup and took a sip. All of a sudden, I found myself rushing to the sink to spit the coffee out of my mouth- realizing that someone had mixed liquid soap into it.

A few mornings later, there was very little water left in the dispenser and I consequently used all of it to make my coffee. I poured myself a cup, and apprehensive after the last incident, carefully measured how much coffee was left in the pot. After a while, I got up to pour out my second cup but observed that the pot contained more coffee than I had left in it. I looked at the water dispenser, and found that it was still empty. That meant that someone had used the water from the sink to refill my coffee pot, despite everyone knowing that it was unsafe to drink.

I had gotten to know of this in the early days after my hiring, when I had gone to the break room to drink water from the sink, and someone had rushed to stop me, saying that it was not safe. Other than that, the bottle of Joy liquid soap clearly states, "For external use only. If taken internally, call poison control immediately." I discussed this with Stan Deloran one day, and he said, "It's harmless. It won't kill you." I could not expect any help from him, yet again.

That makes two counts of attempted murder with two counts of depraved indifference because anybody could have come, drank that coffee and suffered the side effects of being poisoned. All of this seems to have stemmed from me not allowing them to abuse and harass me and treat me like a step and fetch (a slave). To this day, I empty out every pot filled with coffee, before making my own- because I am still traumatized and fear being poisoned.

Chapter 6: Sexual Harassment

On a morning in September 2013, we were assembled for a regular meeting, and one of the union workers- Rafael Rios, filler in packaging- had returned from leave. I said hello to him and stated that I was glad to see him back. Out of nowhere, he grabbed his genitals while looking at me, giving me the finger with his other hand; all the while shouting such vile, disgusting words that I cannot, in good confidence, restate them here. At that point, all I could do is look at him and shake my head with disgust.

Everyone at the meeting had heard him—the supervisor Stan Deloran, Kazi, Alex, and the rest of the lot. I even overheard Kazi saying to Stan, "That's messed up—what Rios did to Brown." And Stan brushed it off, saying that he was just kidding. I found no help there, as always.

I talked to Stan Deloran in the office later, asking

him if he remembered the incident, to which he replied that he did not. To this day, if you ask any of them, they will lie. Someone needs to educate them of the sentencing that perjury carries: three to five years in state or federal prison, from what I know.

Deep down, I always knew I had to tell this story, in order to expose and stop the madness of psychological terrorism and torture in the workplace. Domestic violence is psychological and physical terrorism and torture, as well as violence against another human being. These are serious crimes against the US Constitution on a national and international level, according to articles of the United Nations Assembly.

Chapter 7: Slave Labor/Wage and Hour Violations

The company was utilizing contractors to perform machine operator duties without union-scale pay and membership. The pay rate for a nonunion contractor- which is the job I was hired for- is $17 per hour. On the other hand, the standard pay for machine operators is $26 per hour. That's a nine-dollar difference.

In over two years of me being a machine operator, I was never once paid the amount I was owed. Where was the money going? Was someone pocketing it for themselves?

Moreover, I was the only person sweeping and mopping the packaging warehouse floor for the duration of two years and six months that I worked at Chevron. That makes me the designated industrial custodian, for which the pay is another $17 per hour. Again, I never received even a small cut of this payment.

In addition to these three roles, I was also performing union supervisor duties, which involved training personnel to operate and monitor various machines. The standard pay for this position is $20 per hour. Chevron never paid me a dime for this role either.

I was performing four jobs on my own- the job I was hired for, which was a nonunion-certified forklift warehouseman, a machine operator, a supervisor, and an industrial custodian. All of this without union pay, any benefits, or membership would still amount to a staggering eighty dollars an hour, none of which I was ever paid.

This behavior is a violation of the RICO Act, being unconstitutional, not just nationally, but also according to international law.

Chapter 8: Extortion Conspiracy

I needed to replace my steel-toe work boots one day, so I went into the office to talk to Stan Deloran. He told me that Chevron had contracts with two work boot manufacturers- Red Wing Shoes, and another store whose name escapes me now. Then, he told me that there was a Red Wing Shoes store in Richmond, California.

I explained to him that I would prefer going to the one nearest to my residence in Oakland, California. To that, he assertively responded that I had to go to that particular Red Wing Shoes store. I stated that if Red Wing is a corporation, it must have stores all over the city. But Stan was not to be reasoned with. He told me that if I did not go to that Red Wing store, I would not be able to return to work.

I thought to myself that something does not sound right. So I went there, and I was shocked to find that they had work boots retailed at prices ranging from two hundred to five hundred dollars a pair. I was shocked. I contacted staff mark, where I talked to Laura Trevino and told her about the retail prices for the work boots. She stated, "Yes, I know, but you will receive one hundred fifty dollars back on the price of the boots." Because I really needed them for work, I bought the overly expensive work boots.

A week later, I received the hundred and fifty dollars in my paycheck. That means I only paid fifty dollars for the work boots. I wonder why they didn't just put a fifty dollar price tag on the work boots in the first place? What retail store would prefer to profit from a fifty dollar sale, rather than profit from a two hundred dollar deal? I understand receiving a two or three dollar discount off the retail price, but not a hundred and fifty dollars.

As mentioned before, Stan Deloran had threatened the termination of my contract if I don't buy from that particular branch of Red Wing Shoes. That, to me, is extortion and conspiracy. Red Wing Shoes, Chevron, and staff mark are in a conspiracy of extortion.

Chapter 9: Psychological Terrorism and Torture

These unconstitutional crimes committed against me by my fellow American citizens extend to civil, state, federal, congressional, (RICO) Jim Crow, and international human rights law violations. Psychological terrorism, torture, and warfare are a scientifically proven method to manipulate, control, and/or destroy a person's mind.

Now, I truly know how those people's tortured souls felt at Guantanamo Bay. It does not matter if it is psychological or physical terrorism or torture, the outcome is the same. You cannot physically terrorize and torture people without it affecting them mentally, and you cannot affect them mentally without causing physical harm.

It also targets a person's five senses which allow us to receive information in order to act and function normally in life. But when it comes to people with psychotic minds, this kind of evil is what you must defend yourself against.

That is discrimination, harassment, and retaliation. When you stand up for your rights as a human being with honor and dignity- not only can you find this madness at work, but it is also a part of the system that we live under. Violation of the constitution is domestic treason against government of the United States, as well as the the United Nations assembly charter, European Court of Human Rights, Geneva Conventions, and War crimes tribunals.

The total lack of humanity that I experienced at Chevron was astounding, and no human being should ever have to put up with such evil, psychotic behavior on any job or at any point in their lives. The only way this can change, is if people truly understand just how many rights they have; not only here in the United States, but internationally as well.

Chapter 10: Organized Real Estate Crimes

Before we begin this chapter, let us dive into some basic laws related to real estate and housing in the state of California.

Fair Housing Act, 1968:

This act prohibits discriminatory conduct by a variety of legal entities. The act defines "person" to include one or more individuals, corporations, partnerships, associations, labor organizations, legal representatives, mutual companies, joint-stock companies, trusts, unincorporated organizations, trustees, receivers, and fiduciaries. In addition, municipalities, local government units, cities, and federal agencies are subject to the law. The act explicitly defines a list of prohibited practices involving housing including sales, rentals, advertising, and financing.

Its primary prohibition makes it unlawful to refuse to sell, rent to, or negotiate with any person because of that person's race, color, religion, sex, familial status, handicap, or national origin.

Fair Housing Amendments Act, 1988:

This act added extensive provisions that apply to discrimination against disabled persons and families with children eighteen years of age and under.

Civil Code Section 827:

If you have a month-to-month (or shorter) periodic rental agreement, the landlord must give you at least thirty days' advance written notice of a rent increase.

Landlord Harassment:

The willing creation by a landlord or his agents of conditions that are uncomfortable for one or more tenants in order to induce willing abandonment of a rental contract. Such a strategy is often sought because it avoids costly legal expenses and potential problems with eviction.

Intimidation (also called cowing):

This is an intentional behavior that "would cause a person of ordinary sensibilities" fear of injury or harm. It is not necessary to prove that the behavior was so violent as to cause terror or that the victim was actually frightened.

Extortion:

The obtaining of property from another induced by wrongful use of actual or threatened force, violence, or fear, or under color of official right.

Title 24: Housing and Urban Development:

[Part 100: Discriminatory conducts under the Fair Housing Act Part F-Interference, Coercion, or Intimidation]

- The 24 CFR 100.65: Discrimination in terms, conditions and privileges, and in services
    1. Using different provisions in leases
    2. Failing or delaying maintenance or

repairs of sale or rental

3. Failing to process an offer for the sale or rental (communicate an offer accurately).

- The 24 CFR 100.75: Discriminatory advertisements, statements and notices.

- The 24 CFR 100.400: Prohibited interference, coercion, or intimidation during the twelve months before the rent increase takes effect- upon giving written notice to the tenant, as follows, by either of the following procedures: delivering a copy to the tenant personally and by serving a copy by mail under the procedures prescribed in Section 1013 of the Code of Civil Procedure.

Now that we have understood Californian laws relating to the matter, you can well appreciate the illegality of the following two letters I received from Robert Kramer & Associates, followed by one that I wrote.

Letter #1

Robert Kramer & Associates 585 Mandana Blvd #9 Oakland, CA

FAX (510) 763-9927 TEL (510)763-3850

August 21, 2014

To: All Residents residing at 1826 9th Ave Oakland Ca. 94606 Regarding: Change from Master Electrical Meter to Individual Meters

Dear Residence(s),

This letter is to inform all residents residing at 1826 9th Ave. Oakland that the splitting of the electrical Meters is to be done Monday August 25. 2014, beginning at 8:00 am and ending by 3:00 pm or sooner. The contractors need to shut-off the electricity to complete the work between the hours of 8: am to 3: pm.

The Master Meter will then be eliminated and you will be asked to apply for an account with (1-866-743-2273). Subsequently you will be responsible for payments of your individual electricity usage. We are reducing your rent by $25.00 per-month it's an appropriate consideration. This number has been calculated by taking the past 12-months of the "Electrical Bill" and calculating the average monthly amount and finally dividing by the number of units. Your individual electric billing may be more or less, than the $25.00 reduction in rent based upon the reasons and usage, you will be responsible for paying your individual electric meter billing commencing October 1, 2014.

In the interest of good tenant relationships with our residents, we also prefer to send out the notices of the existence and scope of the City of Oakland's Rent Arbitrators Program.

Please feel free to contact us for any further clarifications or questions at (510)763-3850.

Sincerely,
RK & GG Robert Kramer & Greg Greer
rkarobert@yahoo.com

Letter #2

Robert Kramer & Associates 585
Mandana Blvd #9 Oakland, CA
FAX (510) 763-9927 TEL (510)763-3850

August 21, 2014

To: All Residents residing at 1826 9th Ave Oakland Ca. 94606 Regarding: Change from Master Electrical Meter to Individual Meters

Dear Residence(s),

This letter is to inform all residents residing at 1826 9th Ave. Oakland that the splitting of the electrical Meters is to be done Tuesday September 2. 2014, beginning at 8:00 am and ending by 3:00 pm or sooner. The contractors need to shut-off the electricity to complete the work between the hours of 8: Am to 3: pm.

The Master Meter will then be eliminated and you will be asked to apply for an account with (1-866-743-2273). Subsequently you will be responsible for payments of your individual electricity usage. We are reducing your rent by $25.00 per-month it's an appropriate consideration. This number has been calculated by taking the past 12-months of the "Electrical Bill" and calculating the average monthly amount and finally dividing by the number of units. Your individual electric billing may be more or less, than the $25.00 reduction in rent based upon the reasons and usage, you will be responsible for paying your individual electric meter billing commencing October 1, 2014.

In the interest of good tenant relationships with our residents, we also prefer to send out the notices of the existence and scope of the City of Oakland's Rent Arbitrators Program.

Please feel free to contact us for any further clarifications or questions at (510)763-3850.

Sincerely,

RK & GG Robert Kramer & Greg Greer
rkarobert@yahoo.com

Letter #3

On August 21, 2014, I, Michael Brown, state that the first thirty-day notice of change of terms of tenancy was left at my door, apartment 11, and the doors of the other tenants residing at 1826 Ninth Avenue Oakland, California, 94606.

Then I received a second thirty-day notice of change of terms of tenancy that was left at my door on August 29, 2014. I was not present in the apartment when they left the documents at my door on August 21 and August 29, 2014, and the documents were not mailed to me.

According to the dates on the documents and the attachments, Robert Kramer & Associates violated civil code section 827. You will see where instead of properly delivering the documents to all the tenants at 1826 Ninth Avenue Oakland, California, on August 1, 2014, they illegally and deliberately withheld the documents so they could extort my deposit and the tenants' rent.

The first thirty-day notice of tenancy that was illegally left at my door on August 21, 2014 stated that the meter conversion will take place on August 25, 2014. That's only four days' notice, not thirty days. And the second thirty-day notice of tenancy was illegally left at my door on August 29, 2014, stating that the meter conversion will take place on September 2, 2014. That's only four days' notice, not thirty days, violations of civil code section 827 and 1013 (multiple counts).

I will mail copies of the original documents to the DFEH to compare/authenticate. Robert Kramer & Associates by deliberately violating civil code section 827 and 1013, they have directly violated the Fair Housing Act by using civil code section 827 to extort money and to try and to cover up their illegal activities (under color of official right).

I talked to the head electrician that was doing the meter conversions. He stated the reason they changed the meter conversion from August 25, 2014 to September 2, 2014 is because Robert Kramer & Associates did not want to pay for the extra work rewiring the main electrical system of the apartment complex.

In purposely creating such intimidating and uncomfortable conditions like depriving us- already paying tenant's electricity seven hours a day and withholding the thirty-day notice of tenancy from myself and the ten tenants just because they think they can, is extortion. Under the circumstances when the other ten tenants paid their rent for September 2014, that's extortion (multiple counts).

Because they would have paid their rent under fear of eviction—or a negative credit report reflecting on your credit history may be submitted to a credit reporting agency if you fail to fulfill the terms of your credit obligations— that's intimidation.

I informed Robert Kramer & Associates on August

21, 2014 that I would be moving out because I was unemployed and no longer able to pay the rent. When I rented the apartment over a year ago, it was utility-free rent. But on August 21, 2014, that was the first time I heard about the meter conversion. When I returned to the apartment, I found the first thirty-day notice of tenancy left in my door on August 21, 2014 and the second thirty-day notice of tenancy on August 29, 2014 and in other tenant doors as well. I stated to Robert Kramer & Associates that I need my deposit to survive on because I'm unemployed and homeless. I vacated the premises on September 4, 2014, and they stated that if I leave, I will lose my deposit.

They stated I would be in violation of civil code section 827, and as required by law, you are hereby notified that a negative credit report reflecting on your credit history may be submitted to a credit reporting agency if you fail to fulfill the terms of your credit obligations. According to the document created by the city of Oakland in conjunction with the Department of Fair Housing and

Community Development Rent Adjustment Program and Rent Arbitrators Program, this said documents one of the two pages attached to the thirty-day notice of change of terms of tenancy that Robert Kramer & Associates left at my door, apartment 11, and the doors of the other tenants residing at 1826 Ninth Avenue Oakland, California, 94606 on August 21, 2014 and August 29, 2014 in direct violation of civil code section 827.

It clearly states that the document from the city of Oakland was effective as of August 1, 2014. That means that Robert Kramer & Associates purposely and deliberately withheld the thirty-day notice of change of terms of tenancy from me and the other tenants in order to extort monies from the tenants and myself.

DFEH Case #238332-128161/ FHA SR #2014-9847354

Once again, I reported this to the so-called proper authorities, and they refused to help. I have written this book as my only hope for true justice. Also involved is the city of Oakland because before the real-estate company above could commit the crimes they had to be sanctioned by the city. These case numbers are proof that I have filed with the Department of Fair Housing and Federal Housing Authority.

FBI/EDD Conspiracy

Employment Development Department
PO BOX 12906
OAKLAND, CA 94604-2906

FROM: MICHAEL BROWN

[vader5601@gmail.com]

Order Code 98-326
Report for Congress Received through the CRS Web

SUBJECT: Violations 18 U.S. Code § 2511 - Interception and disclosure of wire, oral, or electronic communications prohibited

18 U.S. Code Chapter 119- Wire And Electronic Communications Interception And Interception Of Oral Communications

18 USC SECTION 241- Conspiracy

18 USC SECTION 242,245 and 42 USC SECTION 1983- Color of Law

Privacy: An Overview of Federal Statutes Governing Wiretapping and Electronic Eavesdropping

Updated January 13, 2003

Gina Stevens, Legislative Attorney
American Law Division

Charles Doyle, Senior Specialist,
American Law Division.

Congressional Research Service,
The Library of Congress

Privacy: An Overview of Federal Statutes Governing Wiretapping and Electronic Eavesdropping Summary

This report provides an overview of federal law governing wiretapping and electronic eavesdropping. It also surveys state law in the area and contains a bibliography of legal commentary.

It is a federal crime to wiretap or to use a machine to capture the communications of others without court approval, unless one of the parties has given their prior consent. It is likewise a federal crime to use or disclose any information acquired by illegal wiretapping or electronic eavesdropping. Violations can result in imprisonment for not more than 5 years; fines up to $250,000 (up to $500,000 for organizations); in civil liability for damages, attorney's fees and possibly punitive damages; in disciplinary action against any attorneys involved; and in suppression of any derivative evidence.

Congress has created separate but comparable protective schemes for electronic mail (e-mail) and against the surreptitious use of telephone call monitoring practices such as pen registers and trap and trace devices. Each of these protective schemes comes with a procedural mechanism to afford limited law enforcement access to private communications and communications records under conditions consistent with the dictates of the Fourth Amendment.

The government has been given even more narrowly confined authority to engage in wiretapping and electronic eavesdropping in the name of foreign intelligence gathering in the Foreign Intelligence Surveillance Act.

I was wrongfully terminated from Staffmark Group LLC and the Chevron oil refinery on 1/31/2014 for whistleblowing on the corrupt activates, because for 2 years and six months, I was subjected to psychological torture/terrorism: in the form of discrimination segregation, favoritism, profiling, stereotyping, harassment, depraved indifference, attempted murder, sexual harassment, slave labor/wage and hour violations, extortion, conspiracy, slavery, kickbacks, violation of the RICO Act, and discrimination.

From May 2011 to January 2014, violations of the Jim Crow laws were also inflicted on me at Chevron Oil Refinery in Richmond Ca, and the FBI has had me and my family's phones under illegal surveillance since I reported the abuses in 2014 and this will prove it. Because, before I filed for my unemployment insurance in 2014 after I was wrongfully terminated I made contact with my supervisor at Staff mark- her name is Laura Trevino, and I stated to her what do you want me to put down on the unemployment benefits application under 'the reason for leaving'? That the contract expired, or that I was psychologically terrorized and tortured? She stated just put down the contract expired.

So when I filed for unemployment I put down the contract expired. So after I filed I received my benefits for 2014. And this is how I know that the FBI has my phone and my families phone tapped. Because when you file for unemployment, EDD is going to check with your last employer to see if the reason for leaving matched what you put down.

On 9-9-2015 I receive a second call from a book publisher regarding publishing my book Psychological Terrorism and he asked me was I still interested in publishing my book. And as I stated before I'm on unemployment insurance. Then he stated to me if we could lower the price to $230.00 per month could I afford it.

Then I stated to him, yes and that I will see what I can do. Then on 9-9-2015 one hour later I received a phone call from a EDD REP at (408) 216-6100 regarding a past claim I filed in 2014 that I applied for and received after I was wrongfully terminated on January 31, 2014 from Staffmark employment and Chevron oil refinery. Stating that Staff mark and chevron oil refinery said that they fired me and not because the contract expired.

I told her no, they wrongfully terminated me because I would not allow them to discriminate, harass and retaliate against me. Then the EDD REP stated that she is going to suspend 2015 EDD unemployment payments until the matter can be straightened out. Then I stated, this is my only means of support. She then stated that it will take a week or longer, so then I stated again how will I survive? She just ignored me.

But as soon as I faxed the EDD REP documents showing that I was discriminated, harassed and retaliated by Staff mark and Chevron Oil and the rest of the conspirator's she reinstated my payments in full.

Now why would the EDD REP decide to check my past unemployment benefit application from 2014 after allocating it to me?

This is how I know that the FBI has my phone tapped. The FBI thought that I was going to use my unemployment benefits to publish my book. So the FBI called EDD and ordered them to stop payments. And my phone is still under surveillance by the FBI as of 2023.

Glossary

Attempted Murder: Attempted murder is the crime of more than merely preparing to commit unlawful killing and at the same time having a specific intention to cause the death of a human being.

Conspiracy: An agreement between two or more persons to commit a crime or accomplish a legal purpose through illegal action.

Depraved Indifference: A person who recklessly engages in conduit that creates a grave risk of death to another person and thereby causes serious physical injuries to that person or to a third person.

Extortion: An excessive or exorbitant charge.

Favoritism: The practice of giving unfair preferential treatment to one person or group at others' expense.

Harassment: A feeling of intense annoyance caused by being tormented.

Kickbacks: An amount of money that is given to someone in return for providing help in a secret and dishonest business deal.

Profiling: The practice of categorizing people.

Psychological Terrorism/Torture: A scientific method in which you attempt to psychologically manipulate control or destroy a person's mind and will through the use of terrorism and torture. It also targets a person's five senses, because you receive information through your five senses.

Rico Act: The RICO Act was passed by the United States Congress to enable persons financially injured by a pattern of criminal activity to seek redress through the state or federal courts.

Segregation: The action or state of separation, isolation.

Sexual Harassment: The harassment of any person in a workplace or other professional or social situation, involving the making of unwanted sexual advances or obscene remarks.

Slave/Labor/Wage and Hour Violations: The Fair Labor Standards Act (FLSA) protects workers from being deprived of fair payment by their employers for their time. The most common wage and hour violations occur in high-tech industries, food industry jobs, construction jobs, and hotel jobs.

Stereotyping: One that is regarded as embodying or conforming to a set image or type.

Terrorism: The unlawful use or threatened use of force or violence by a person or an organized group against people or property with the intention of intimidating or coercing societies or governments, often for ideological or political reasons.

www.ingramcontent.com/pod-product-compliance
Lightning Source LLC
LaVergne TN
LVHW010606070526
838199LV00063BA/5091